How to Sell a Screenplay in the 21ˢᵗ Century

Vol.5 of the ScriptBully Screenwriting Collection

by Michael Rogan
Editor, ScriptBully Magazine

Published in USA by: ScriptBully Magazine

Michael Rogan

© Copyright 2018

ISBN-13: 978-1-970119-04-6
ISBN-10: 1-970119-04-7

Table of Contents

About the Author

Michael Rogan is a former Hollywood screenplay reader, optioned screenwriter and editor of ScriptBully magazine - an inbox periodical devoted to helping screenwriters write well...and get paid.

He is also the owner of the world's most neurotic Jack Russell Terrier.

And has made it his mission in life to rid the world of movies about trucks that turn into robots.

A Special FREE Gift for You!

If you'd like FREE instant access to my seminar "7 Secrets to a Kick-Ass and Marketable Screenplay" then head over to **ScriptBully.com/Free**. (What else you gonna do? Watch another "Twilight" movie?!)

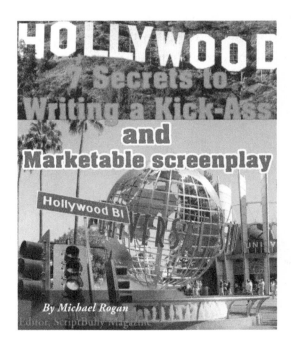

Prologue: "Never Tell Me the Odds"

"Ah, but a man's reach should exceed his grasp, or what's a heaven for?"

-Robert Browning

You're not going to believe what I'm about to say.

It's okay. I get it. You're a screenwriter.

Skepticism comes with the territory. Like bitter angst and an obsessive film noir DVD collection.

The truth is: There has never been a better time to get your screenplay read, noticed and ultimately sold.

It's just nobody in the business wants you to know it.

"This Is NOT a Boat Accident"

I could tell you it's the unprecedented power of social media to make connections with film industry decision-makers.

Or that the line between content creator and distributor is as thin as a Russian supermodel's waistline.

Or that the systematic collapse of the traditional publishing paradigm has redefined what a "published" property is, making any self-published novel, eBook or blog — fertile ground for the start of a bidding war.

But, really, I think it's that nobody in this business knows what the hell "media" will look like in the future.

Are we STILL going to go to movies in five years? Ten years? Next week?

Will movies need to be shot for mobile devices,

not just for your local Cineplex 3-D projector? (And what the hell will cell phones look like?)

And will there still be a window between the time a movie is released theatrically and when it arrives on your TV/DVR/Blu-Ray Player/Robot Brain?

Nobody knows.

And that scares the hell out of everybody who works in this town.

Because it means the folks who distribute and develop content can't instantly say "no" to every project that comes in the door.

It means they can't assume the best material out there comes from writers with overpriced USC film-school educations.

"Julie and Julia" grossed 94 million dollars, and was based on a mundane, self-indulgent food blog.

"Fifty Shades of Grey" started out as a "Twilight" message-board vanity project and quickly created one of the biggest bidding wars in Hollywood. (You have no idea what kind of final approval the writer got for that deal.)

Colleen Houck couldn't give away her young adult novel "Tiger's Curse" to anybody in the publishing industry. So, she self-pub'd it on Amazon. (Paramount Pictures - the studio that made "The Godfather" — bought it and immediately put it into development.)

To feed the ever-demanding content beast, development people need you.

They just hate admitting it.

Why the Film Business Hates You

As a writer, you are a major time suck.

You take up their weekends, with your 123-page sprawling historical epics and your sci-fi fantasy yarns.

You force them to write extensive pages of reader coverage, to prove to their bosses why you suck.

You squander their time with your annoying

phone calls and misspelled query letters and stalker-ish questions at conference Q&As.

And if they like what you wrote that's when the major time suckage really starts.

That means they've gotta devote months, if not years, fighting for you on studio lots and pitching your talent to bipolar actors & insufferable directors.

So, the last thing they want to do is say yes.

But they also know there is the slightest, remote chance that the next script that plops on their desk - your script - might be the next "Hurt Locker" or "Bridesmaids" or "Paranormal Activity 14 1/2".

And to have the chance to be a part of a project like that is what everybody - even the most cynical, jaded, coked-out, sex-addicted development person - dreams of.

"Take Your Stinkin' Paws Off Me, You Damned Dirty Ape!"

When selling your script, you will hear the word "no."

You will feel you're the worst writer in the world.

You will get hung up on and ignored and told you should give up your dreams and, instead, get a job at your local Orange Julius.

Don't worry. It's just noise.

If your script is awesome and unique - and I'll go over how to get it there in a later chapter - then it WILL capture the attention of somebody who can jump-start your career and change your life.

Finding that somebody is what this book is all about.

Chapter 1:
How to Conquer Hollywood 3,000 Miles Away

"The life you have led doesn't have to be the only one you have."

-Anna Quindlen

John Wanamaker, marketing guru and overall cool guy, once said:

"Half the money I spend on advertising is a waste of money. Trouble is: I don't know which half."

Most of the action steps in this book won't work. They won't lead to substantive leads.

Trouble is: we've no idea which steps those are.

You've got to throw everything against the wall and see which email query and festival pitch fest sticks.

You've got to have a mindset, as the Persian poet Rumi opined, that is: "Open to everything, and attached to nothing."

And, believe me, there's a whole lot of "nothing" in Hollywood.

"She Was a Junkie for the Printed Word"

This is how most screenwriting books suggest you approach selling your script:

- Buy a copy of the "Hollywood Creative Directory."

- Send out 150-200 query letters to agents and managers.

- Hope for a 10 percent positive response rate.

- Send out 15-20 scripts for consideration.

- Hope one of them buys your script.

- Rinse and Repeat.

This might have worked back in the Mesozoic era (or as I like to call it, 1995), but things move a whole lot faster now.

For starters:

- The "Hollywood Creative Directory" no longer exists.

- Query letters are a joke. (No one I know in production reads them anymore.)

- Agents and managers (most likely) won't have anything to do with you until you have talent attached to your project.

I suggest a more holistic, 21st Century approach in which you do the following simultaneously:

- Come up with a kick-ass script idea.

- Create a database of above-the-line talent (producers, actors, directors, etc.) for every film in your genre that was released in the last two years.

- Write your script.

- Use Facebook, Twitter and YouTube to build out your social network and list of contacts.

- Rewrite your script.

- Attend every film festival and conference you can possibly afford.

- Rewrite your script. (Again.)

- Collect the names of agents and managers who represent the above-the-line contacts you've amassed.

- Send out your SHORT query BY EMAIL to relevant industry folk in your genre.

- Follow up with a phone call and schmooze the receptionist.

- Send out your script.

- Sell your script.

- Celebrate with a Mai Tai on a Polynesian island.*

(*Last one is optional. You may choose any tropical island you prefer.)

"Are You Ready for a War?"

But to amass your list of contacts, and be seen as a professional even if you're living in an igloo in Nova Scotia, you will need some tools of the trade.

So like the Act-II Climax of every Steven Seagal movie, let's go get you a rocket launcher and prepare you for script-selling battle:

Tool No. 1: IMDb Pro (Paid)

Here's a fun quiz: Want to know if a screenwriting book is out of date? See if they recommend buying the "Hollywood Creative Directory" (HCD).

The HCD was, for years, the go-to manual for finding contact info on anybody in the entertainment business. (Hell, I've got three of them sitting on my bookshelf right now.)

It was also expensive. ($185 for the print version, well over $300 for the online subscription.)

But, with that pesky thing called the Internet, tracking down info on Christina Ricci's manager got a hell of a lot cheaper. Which put the HCD out of business. (Even their website is gone. Sad, sad.)

Instead, buy a subscription to IMDb Pro. It costs $124.95 a year (or $15.95/month); well worth the price of admission to a career as a screenwriter.

Yes, it's possible to scour message boards and pitch festivals for contact info for managers and agents representing the talent you want attached to your script.

But really, wouldn't that time be better spent writing your action-comedy spec than finding contact info for Gary Busey's manager?

Tip: If you're dirt poor, likely, if you're a writer, try the 2-week free trial of IMDb Pro and collect all your phone numbers and email addresses without paying a single dime.

Tool No.2: L.A. Phone Number (Free)

After you've sold your first script, you can churn out screenplays from a mud hut in Bangladesh for all Hollywood cares. But until then: You've gotta be perceived as someone "in town."

And there's NO better way to do that, without moving here, than to sign up for a Google Voice account. This allows you to set up a phone number with a 310, 323, 424 or 818 area code.

Not only will it let you forward calls from your new number to any number you want — cell, home, work, payphone, carrier pigeon, etc. — but you can listen in while the person is leaving a message. (And you get an email text transcript of each call to your Gmail account. Way cool.)

Tool No.3: Clever Business Cards (Paid...But So Cheap They're Not Worth Worrying About)

In a later chapter, I'll dig into how attending film festivals and writer conferences is key to meeting people who can get your script read. (And sold.) But for now, know you will need business cards to swap.

These are not the cards from your day job. NOT: "Jim Myers: Screenwriter/Masseuse/Waste Treatment Manager."

Make it a screenwriting only business card.

Whatever design you choose, make sure it's got:

- Your L.A. Google Voice phone number

- Email (Please no SupaFly34@hotmail.com, use something with your real, or pen, name)

- Facebook Page (Optional)

- Twitter (Optional, but highly recommended)

- Website: (Optional)

Tool No.4: The Ability to Talk to Humans (Free or Paid)

I know you became a writer because you're shy and reserved.

And you hate all living beings and want to while away the hours in your New Hampshire cottage penning screenplays about injustice and the death of nuance.

Sorry, Salinger, but the film biz doesn't work that way.

You need other people to turn your screenplay into a work of art. And "other people" don't sit around thinking: "Boy, I wonder which isolated, socially-awkward writer in southern Idaho I should contact today?"

You've gotta get on people's radar. And to do that you've gotta talk to people in a relaxed and confident way.

Now, you don't have to be George Clooney, or Rosemary Clooney for that matter. But you must be able to walk up to somebody at a film festival and introduce yourself.

Or call a production company up on the phone and ask for the name of their story editor, without sounding like a nineteen-year-old telemarketer selling car insurance.

If it means buying a Tony Robbins DVD series or taking an acting class or completing a reincarnation mantra weekend...do it!

You'll thank me when you collect a down payment for your New Hampshire cottage.

Chapter 1 Key Takeaways:

- **There are some key resources every would-be professional screenwriter needs to have in their promotional toolbox.** And the now-defunct "Hollywood Creative Directory" is not one.

- **The most important resource is a subscription to IMDb Pro.** This will give you contact info for tons of managers and agents of actors and directors. (If you're really broke, you could sign up for FREE trials through different email addresses.)

- **The second key resource is an L.A. phone number.** This can be easily accomplished by signing up for a Google Voice account and creating a phone number with a 310 or 213 area code.

- **Another vital part of your screenwriter**

toolkit is a halfway decent business card. Be sure to include your L.A. phone number, email and any social media writer profiles you have. (Make sure it's for screenwriting only.)

- **The final piece to the puzzle is the ability to converse with humans in a (somewhat) comfortable way**. Don't worry if you're scared; everyone is scared. Just fake it till you make it — or the medication kicks in.

Chapter 2:
Is Your Script Ready for Prime-Time?

"An invasion of armies can be resisted, but not an idea whose time has come."

-Victor Hugo

I will assume, if you're reading this book, you've already finished a full-length screenplay. (Something between 90-115 pages)

I'm gonna also assume it doesn't suck and is awesome. And by awesome, your script contains:

A main character who MUST do something they don't want to do or else this other REALLY BAD THING will happen. (Translation: dilemma!)

A main character forced to do something WAY outside their comfort zone.

At least three set pieces. These can be: exciting car chases, amazing verbal battles, climactic showdowns, outrageous comedic sequences.

A strong antagonist that is way, way stronger than your hero. (Can be Darth Vader. An oppressive city hall. Killer teddy bears.)

A cool, ironic premise, that hasn't been done to death. (Senior citizens forced to defend their residence center from ninjas; Fashion designer forced to work the clothing rack at Wal-Mart when she violates probation, etc.)

At least three rewrites on your script.

If you haven't checked these off of your to-do list, please go back and do so. Then come on back.

Don't worry. I'll be here.

"Ever Dance With the Devil By the Pale Moonlight?"

So if you've done the above, that must mean you're ready to drop your script off with the receptionist at CAA, right?

Eh...not quite.

First, we've gotta bulletproof your script. Like Broadway productions that open in Buffalo, we need to give your script a test drive to make sure it's got its sea legs.

And, we'll accomplish this in the ScriptBully 3-Phase "Make Your Script Awesome" Process:

Script Awesomeness Phase No.1: Get a Second (and a Third and a Fourth...) Opinion

Compile a list of five people to read your script. They don't have to be in the industry. (In fact, they probably shouldn't be.)

These can be friends. Family. Your dentist. The

homeless guy who sells newspapers on your street corner.

They just need to be movie fans. Not somebody who last went to the theatre to see "Titanic". ("I just LOVED that Celine Dion song!")

And they need to know crap when they see it.

My dad, who walked out of "G.I. Joe" saying "that was better than 'Star Wars'," would not be somebody I would approach.

My wife who "hates romantic comedies where girls are ALWAYS clumsy" might be a better choice.

"Fasten Your Seatbelts. It's Going to Be a Bumpy Night"

Bribery gets such a bad rap. Which is unfortunate, because it's staggeringly effective. (Especially at getting folks to read your script.)

Be sure if you ask ANYBODY to read your script, you bribe them with something tangible to show appreciation for their time and effort. Reading a script can be a total pain and you want to make sure they actually do it. (Bottles of wine are good, so are free dinners. Dates with Scarlett Johansson work remarkably well.)

Whatever you do, please print out the script. Don't make them read it on a laptop. It's lame and you'll get crappy feedback.

Also, be sure to ask them to be honest. You are not looking for approval. (That's what your therapist is for.)

You want REAL feedback. Don't worry, you probably won't get it, but you'll get what people like and don't like.

And if you do get the same critical note from two different people, then you'll know you've got something to work on.

Take all the feedback and rewrite those areas until your script is exactly where you want it. Then you can move on to...

Script Awesomeness Phase 2: Hit the Stage

I'm shocked how many writers don't use this (virtually) free method for improving their script. This will boost your script's quality by 150 percent.

So, here's what you do. Contact your regional theatre company or junior college theatre department and tell them you've just finished a feature-length screenplay.

Ask them if you could organize a staged reading before submitting the material to L.A. production companies.

They will practically fall over themselves to help you.

First, most actors are looking for any excuse to perform in public. And second, hearing you will be "submitting" to Hollywood will get anybody excited. ("Maybe this guy can help my career…"; "Perhaps I can quit my job at the Reno Starbucks and move to Cal-i-forni-a.")

A few things to keep in mind:

- Record the event with good audio. (This will be priceless later.)

- Pay attention to when people laugh.

- Pay attention to when actors stumble over lines. (This is where you've probably written awkward dialogue or description.)

- Pay attention to when you get bored. (You will. Trust me.)

- Be sure to provide plenty of drinks and snacks. (Nothing more heartless than not paying an artist for their craft.)

- When you finish, take the recording and listen to it. Over and over and over.

What you thought was a scene full of taut action, actually has all the energy and passion of an HR orientation.

Remove it. Rewrite it. Make it more awesome. When you do that, you're ready for...

Phase No.3: Calling In the Professionals

You should, by this point, have made some serious improvements to your script. (Most notably, making it way shorter and less boring.)

Now it's time to approach a professional, or semi-professional, or at least somebody who can give you more constructive feedback than "I don't care for the name Maxine."

If you've got a friend in the industry, this is when you reach out.

Don't ask for help to sell it. Don't ask them to hand it to Chris Nolan or deliver it via carrier pigeon to Hilary Swank.

Just tell them you want to see how it stacks up to industry-standard screenplays. See how that request takes the pressure off and gives them a clearly defined objective.

But...what do you do if you know nobody in the biz?

Here are a couple of ideas:

Pro Reader Option No.1: Get a Script Consultant to Read Your Script

I know a lot of people look down on this method, but for a couple hundred bucks this can be a great way to find out how you stack up against all the other newbies who are submitting.

There are tons of great consultants. (Linda Seger, Michael Hauge, and John Rainey are a couple of the best. But they are not cheap.) Try not to spend more than $500.

(Special offer: I rarely take on new clients; I spend most of my time writing little books like this one. But as a thank you for checking out my book you can get a discount on my script consulting services. Just email me at michael@scriptbully.com with the Discount Coupon code SCRIPTREADER and we'll try to set something up.)

Pro Reader Option No.2: Reach Out to a Production Company

One way to get a professional eye on your script is to reach out to a story editor or development executive at a production company and see if they would, for 300 bucks, read your script.

Again, reiterate you're not looking to make a sale. You've enjoyed their work - whatever those credits may be - and you want to see how your work stacks up in the industry.

Someone will jump at this. (Probably the most underpaid member of the story department.) And, best of all, if your script kicks ass, they'll probably want to buy it. (And then having dinner with Scarlett Johansson suddenly gets a lot more likely.)

Chapter 2 Key Takeaways:

- **Try to get at least FIVE people to read your script.** They don't have to be professionals, just movie fans. Thank them with a bottle of their favorite beverage. Any notes mentioned twice need work.

- **Organize a staged reading with your local theatre department** to get a crash-course education in what works — and doesn't work. (Don't forget the bagels!)

- **Getting a professional reader to look over your script can be a worthwhile investment.** (Don't spend more than $500). Places to look for readers include production companies and professional script consultants.

Chapter 3:
How to Make Your Story Not Sound Sucky

"He who cannot limit himself will never know how to write."

-Nicholas Boileau

They call 'em elevator pitches.

Those quick summaries of a business idea that corporate types give to each other to raise investment capital, increase brand awareness and sell the world some shitty app it doesn't need.

The reason it's called an elevator pitch is that it takes, on average, 118 seconds for an elevator to travel from the ground floor to the top floor of most hotels.

And this, the left-brain types figure, is the perfect time for you to talk about your new start-up.

If only you had that much time as a writer.

Really, you've got about five seconds. Ten, if I'm feeling generous. (Which, I'm not.)

Doesn't matter if you're writing an email to a producer or phoning up an agent — no query letters, that's so 1998 — you've got to get to your idea fast. Quicker than fast.

Light speed.

Grab people instantly with your story idea. And this means knowing what the hell your story idea is.

I touched on it briefly, but here's the formula I recommend to my screenwriting tribe:

Your pitch is a PERSON who MUST do a thing or else this OTHER REALLY BAD THING will happen.

But here's the wrinkle:

- The MUST has to be the last thing they want to do.

- The GOAL, or avoidance of pain, has to be personal.

- The GOAL has to be tangible and concrete. (Andy in "Shawshank Redemption" doesn't just want freedom; he wants to live in Mexico and sail on his boat.)

- The MUST has got to be strong, ironic and supremely hard.

- The PREMISE has to be something we haven't seen before.

This would not qualify:

A mild-mannered librarian must re-categorize the over-sized book collection of her branch or else a fourth-grade class won't be able to do their book reports.

Problems:

- The stakes are low.
- The thing she's gotta do is not easy and/or outside her comfort zone.
- There's no sense of irony.
- The core idea radically blows.

This one is also a no-go:

When a lounge singer witnesses a gangland murder, she must enter a convent to avoid being killed by the Mob.

The premise is good. But unless you plan on rebooting the whole "Sister Act franchise" — they've rebooted the "Hulk" property about twelve times, so ya never know — then you gotta move on to something else.

These would work better:

A mild-mannered librarian must travel back in time to a

dangerous land to rescue Shakespeare from an evil warlord or all of western civilization perishes.

Or...

A mild-mannered librarian must enter a beauty pageant to track down her best friend's killer.

Or...

A mild-mannered librarian must enter a Muay Thai death-match tournament to rescue her kidnapped father.

Or...

A mild-mannered librarian must work as a stripper to find an undiscovered Shakespeare play.

I'm not suggesting these are awesome. But they have high stakes, at least for the character. And they have a sense of opposites. (Librarians doing very un-librarian things.)

So I'll ask you? Pretend I'm pitching these to you. Which do you like better?

Personally, I like the stripper one. It seems like that would require the main character to "travel" the most, both physically, emotionally and VISUALLY.

So...how can we make it more personal? More relatable?

How about:

A mild-mannered librarian must go undercover as a stripper to rescue her runaway younger sister.

Now we're talking.

This instantly conjures up lots of good conflict. With the fellow strippers, with the sleazy club owner, with her uptight fiance who threatens to leave her, with her own sister, with her parents who might blame her for the way things turned out and, most of all, with herself.

Chapter 3 Key Takeaways:

- **The ideal story pitch is short, focused and ironic**. If it doesn't sound like a movie you would pay for, keep reworking.

- **A good formula for your pitch** is: "A [somebody] who must [do something they don't want to do] or else [this even worse something will happen.]

- **Common flaws include a premise that's NOT original, emotional or goal-oriented**. Keep it simple…but powerful.

- **Pitch your story to as many people as will physically listen**. Notice their reactions — when they seem interested, when they seemed bored. And keep working on it until fellow writers shake their head in jealousy.

Chapter 4:
How NetFlix Can Help You Sell Your Script

"The two most powerful warriors are patience and time."

-Leo Tolstoy

I love "Colombo."

And "Rockford Files." And "Quincy." And "Vegas." (Something about late 70's procedural drama and a glass of Pinot Noir is my idea of blissed-out Nirvana.)

But when I'm trying to sell a script, I realize

there are only so many hours in the day. And everything I watch needs to have a purpose.

And while watching a cop show written in 1978 can be a helpful reminder of how to "break" story, it won't help me get my current horror spec script sold.

Fortunately, or unfortunately, going to the movie theater to watch "Hostel 7: Attack of the Co-Op Housing Killer," just might.

"Von Trapp Children Don't Play, They March"

The secret to finding someone to "read" and act on your script is to find somebody who can "use" your script to propel his/her own career to the next level.

And the people who are most desperate for an occupational turbo-boost are ascending talent, not established players in the biz.

Derek Cianfrance may have read your erotic thriller script before he helmed "Blue Valentine," but not after.

Emma Stone might have looked at your romantic comedy before "Easy A," but not now.

Jennifer Lawrence might have possibly looked at your action spec before "The Hunger Games," but you sure as shit can't get her on the phone now.

And how do you find those eager, hungry talents?

The formula is simple:

- Watch as many movies as you can within your genre that were made in the last two years. (The more independent, the better. Netflix is great for this.)

- Write down the key players for each movie (producers, directors, actors, etc.)

- Find their contact info, or their rep's contact info, in IMDb Pro and add them to your spreadsheet of choice.

- Contact them.

But to do this you've gotta get off your ass and go see some movies in your genre, before they play them on TBS on a Saturday afternoon in between showings of "Beastmaster."

You've gotta scroll through your Netflix queue and find all the obscure, indie films in your genre before Robert Osborne presents them on Turner Classic Movies.

You've gotta know which studios and production companies produce which kinds of films. (New Line loves horror and Tyler Perry films. Disney, well...doesn't even make movies anymore.)

It's all fine and good to watch "The Shawshank Redemption" for the fifteenth time when you've sold your script.

But when you're in sell mode, you've gotta stay focused. You've gotta watch new(ish) films made by people looking for a better office on the Paramount lot.

You've gotta find folks as ambitious and hungry

as yourself.

"This IS a Tasty Burger"

I know you're busy. I know you have no time.

I know you've (probably) got a soul-draining job that eats all your free time.

But I'd like you to see at least three new (ish) movies in your genre per week, one in the theatre and two on Netflix or HBO or whatever.

If there are no movies in your genre available at your local Cineplex, see something else. (Horror/suspense and low-budget rom-coms are always good breeding grounds for new talent. Action movies, not so much.)

For each film, I'd like you to add the following peeps to your database:

- Producer

- Co-Producer

- Interesting Actors That Don't Suck and are Relatively Unknown

- Newbie(ish) Directors

- The D.P. or Director of Photography

- The Studio

- The Production Company

A few thoughts on these:

Producers

Of the above people to contact, my absolute favorites are producers. These are the people who spend years (sometimes decades) finding material and birthing it from development to DVD sales. They are also some of the craziest, most awesome (and awful) people on the planet.

Don't worry so much about executive producers. These are usually money people. And forget line producers, who are not generally involved in the creative side.

Co-producers, however, usually bring in the name actors. These are good people to know. Which can make them a valuable addition to your database.

Actors

Actors are the FASTEST way into this biz. (Or more accurately, through their agent or manager.) But you've gotta get them early. Putting Channing Tatum or Jennifer Lawrence on your list NOW is a waste of time.

And you've gotta make sure your material is a fit. (Think where they want to be, not where they are right now.)

Or better yet, think of where they USED to be. There's no one as motivated as a washed-up thespian in need of a career resurrection. (Read: John Travolta in "Pulp Fiction.")

My favorite genre for this is Slasher films.

(Especially actresses.)

There are always one or two talented women in a horror movie who you can tell are better than the material and are just hoping for that breakout script to get them out of Gore-ville. (Maybe your breakout script?)

Directors

Directors can be the most difficult to reach. But they are also the quickest way to get a project green-lit.

Studios feel way more comfortable knowing a good director is on board than a comparably good actor. (Oh, how things have changed.)

But, as with actors, you have to reach 'em on the way up. (I love finding semi-obscure directors on Netflix. There are TONS on there.)

And don't forget the D.P. or Director of Photography. Aside from a few F-Stop junkies who don't want to do anything but cinematography, most D.P.s would love a shot at helming a feature.

Studios and Production Companies

You won't be contacting studios directly. But keeping track of which studio produced or distributed a film is a good way to learn who makes what in this town.

Production companies, on the other hand, are a veritable goldmine for a screenwriter.

Yes, they are often affiliated with the producer, or assistant producer on a project, but "prod-cos" also have in-house story editors and development executives who you can add to your list and contact later.

Chapter 4 Key Takeaways:

- **Watching movies in your chosen genre,** made in the last five years, is a key part of your screenwriting craft. Try watching three films per week. (As homework goes, it's pretty damn fun.)

- **For each film you watch, gather relevant contact info** from the credits (producer, co-producer, line producer, director, DP, actors, studio, production company). You can then look up their rep's contact info on IMDb Pro.

- **Producers and co-producers can be great contacts** to add to your list. Forget line producers and executive producers. (It's unlikely they'll read your script.)

- **For finding actors to contact be sure to look for "rising" talent** who can be helped by your script. TV shows and slasher films are great places to find emerging acting talent in need of a great script.

- **Directors — and would-be directors in the form of 2nd-unit directors and D.P.'s (Director of Photography)** — can be a great way to attach serious talent to your script. Be sure to contact their manager or agent and not the director directly.

Chapter 5:
How Festivals and Conferences Can Make You Moolah

"Success goes to the ones who do. Do it afraid, but do it no matter."

-Toni Sorenson

Again, I know. Talking to total strangers is the last thing you want to do.

But film festivals and writer conferences are some of the best places to meet industry people because:

- People there love films. (Usually.)

- People can't hide behind an email address.

- You (sometimes) get the chance to pitch your story.

- Most writers are too shy or too obnoxious to make a good impression, so you stand out.

Be cool, and keep your expectations moderately low, and this can be a phenomenal way to sneak past the gatekeepers.

"You'll Never Find a More Wretched Hive of Scum and Villainy"

Writer conferences are equal parts MFA-program and script idea cattle call. And that's okay.

Just make sure you spend plenty of time in the hotel bar.

That's where you'll meet the development executives and producers in a more laid-back setting.

If you appear chill (read: not creepy), then you might get a business card that can change your life.

Here are a couple of tips to make sure you kill it at your next writer's conference:

- *Tip No.1:* **Choose conferences that specialize in screenwriting.** I give suggestions at the end of this chapter, but just know you should skip the Writer's Digest and Fiction Writer Heaven conferences for when you write your memoir. Keep it focused on film.

- *Tip No.2:* **Find out who the panelists and/or industry types are beforehand.** This isn't always possible, but a key to success is knowing who you're talking to (what their credits are) and knowing what they look like. (Creepy? Maybe. Effective? Yes.)

- *Tip No.3:* **Record every Q&A, panel, and seminar you attend.** You never know when they'll say something you can use, such as "finding a good romantic comedy is like drilling for oil," in an email query later.

- *Tip No.4:* **Dress casual, but cool.** Dump the NASCAR t-shirts and the suit and tie. Keep it hip, but not like you're trying to be hip. Blazers and jeans are good for men. For women...uh...something nice?

- *Tip No.5:* **Pitch as much as you can.** Many conferences will offer you the chance to pitch your story idea, usually for a small fee. Do this. Many times. It may seem stupid, but it's great practice and you might just hit it off with one exec.

- *Tip No.6:* **Don't be THAT asshole in the audience** who asks the self-serving question to the panel trying to show off your film knowledge. Yes, you've seen every version of "Touch of Evil" on Blu-Ray. That does not make you a part of the film industry.

"Here's the Pitch..."

So you signed up for one of those pitch fests. What the hell do you do now?

Well, I find the most difficult part for writers is getting started with their pitch. Shifting from small talk to full-on pitch mode.

Example:

"Hi, John Walker, famous development executive for DreamWorks. Great to meet you. I can't name any movies you've done, but I'm sure they were good. (Pause) So...shall I start?

"Okay, I'll start...

"We fade in on the Mojave desert. A group of ninja strippers prepare to attack a water treatment center..."

Wow. That's awkward.

Instead, take a cue from one of the best pitching experts out there, Michael Hauge.

There are few great books on pitching, Michael's book, "<u>Selling Your Story in 60 Seconds</u>" has got some great pitch templates in there for a variety of scenarios. I highly recommend you pick up a copy.

The technique Michael suggests, and I endorse, is to simply start with some small talk, then move on to how you came up with the idea.

THEN get on with your story idea.

So if I would pitch somebody I'd do something like this:

"Hi, Jim. Like you, I'm a Clippers fan, so I know what it's like to be a supporter of lost causes." (Shows I'm funny, and I did my homework. And I'm not a robot.)

"So, I guess the best way for me to get the ball rolling is to tell you how I came up with the idea for my script. One day, the water went off at my house. And I thought...hmmm. Did I not pay my bill? Or was it ninjas? Or, better yet, ninja strippers?"

See how much more organically the conversation flows?

As for what should be in the pitch itself: This will be more than just the elevator pitch we worked on earlier. You're face-to-face. You can do more.

I would break it down this way:

Start with when and where...and be sure to add a twist:

"It's 1868. The Civil War is over. A small South Carolina town finds itself with no living male citizens under the age of 60. And way too many werewolves."

Then the set up:

"The town appoints a reluctant, retired and crippled Confederate Colonel as sheriff. But he gets more than he bargained for when he finds out the town is in the warpath of a werewolf army."

Then your second-act climax:

"After battling the werewolves, and losing his wife in an attack, he's captured. Only to find out his 'deceased' Confederate soldier son is the one leading the undead werewolf attack.

Then your resolution:

"The sheriff must raise the 'Union Army dead' - his sworn enemies - to defeat his son's werewolf pack in a climactic battle that forces him to question honor, family and the sins of the past."

That's it. If they ask questions, and want more info, those are really good things.

Don't go on and on about the hair color of the hero or which actor would be great for it or your favorite scenes or how they can read a copy if they want. (Of course they can. That's why you're there.) Be quick. Be stealthy. Be like a ninja. (Or at the very least, a ninja stripper.)

It's a Festival Thang

So we've gone over conferences. Now let's turn to film festivals. (At the end of this chapter, I suggest a couple of festivals worth checking out.)

Festivals are a little more chaotic and require a bit more chutzpah. But when it comes to meeting ambitious, young directors and actors, there may be no better venue to ply your wares.

Here are a couple of things to help you make the most of your experience:

Tip No.1: **Remember it's all about them.**
Most people are there to win awards and get laid.
Ask them about their projects, what they're there to
see, what they're doing next. (You'll stand out from
most of the other schmoozers and talent barnacle
that show up at these things.)

Tip No.2: **Don't sell.** You aren't there to get
somebody to read your script. You're there to get a
shitload of business cards, which can turn into
contacts. Which can later turn into readers. Don't
shrink-wrap the process.

Tip No.3: **See lots of movies.** It's good for
your craft. It's good for your ability to find out who's
doing what in which movie. It's good for your
confidence to see how much utter crap there is out
there.

Tip No.4: **Seek out films with Q&As.** These
are great for finding out what material directors are
drawn to, and what actors like about a certain
project. (Just like in the Netflix chapter, write down
all the principals you can.)

Tip No.5: **Talk to people in line.** You never
know who's next to you. Tell them what you've seen
and liked so far. Or what you're excited to see. Be

nice. Be interesting. Be human. (I know you can do it.)

Tip No.6: **Sleep when you're dead.** Go out at night to all the bars and cool places where people are hanging out. Too shy? Just walk up and say: "Which film are you starring in?" People just love to be mistaken for actors.

Super Sneaky Festival Networking Secret

I know you're not going to be able to go to every conference and festival on the face of the earth.

But here's a super sneaky way to still get something out of every fest or conference, even the ones you miss:

Secret No.1: Collect Them Names

Get the list of every producer, story editor, or development exec who attends a pitch fest or panel at a writer's conference or film festival. (Usually available on the festival websites.)

What does their attendance at that fest tell you? It tells you they, or their company, are looking for material. Add them to your spreadsheet and you can query them later.

Secret No.2: Watch the Recording

Most conferences and festivals will either put their panels on YouTube, iTunes or possibly sell them as bundled recordings. Watch and listen to as many as you can. This will put you in the room, without having to have paid the airfare.

Writer's Conferences That Don't Suck

The ones I've been to personally and can highly recommend are:

- Austin Film Festival/Screenwriting Conference (Austin, TX) http://www.austinfilmfestival.com/

- Nashville Screenwriting Conference (Nashville, TN)

http://www.nashscreen.com/

Other ones I've heard good things about are:

- Toronto Screenwriting Conference (Toronto, ON) http://www.torontoscreenwritingconference.com/

- Stonybrook Summer Conference (Stony Brook, NY) http://www.stonybrook.edu/sb/mfa/summer/screenwriting/

I know these can be a huge expense, sometimes hundreds of dollars (not including airfare and lodging.) But I'd recommend you squeeze in at least one of these a year.

Film Festivals That Don't Suck

There are so many, it's tough to pick just a few. Many also have corresponding screenplay contests.

But here are some of my faves:

- Sundance Film Festival
  http://www.sundance.org/festival/

- Telluride Film Festival
  http://telluridefilmfestival.org/

- South by Southwest http://sxsw.com/

- Slamdance Film Festival
  http://www.slamdance.com/

- Austin Film Festival
  http://www.austinfilmfestival.com/

- Tribeca Film Festival
  http://www.tribecafilm.com/festival/

Chapter 5 Key Takeaways:

- **Try to attend at least one screenwriter conference and one film festival this year.** Record the panels, get lots of business cards and pitch your story until your voice goes hoarse.

- **Start off your pitch with HOW you came up with the idea of your script.** Don't RUSH in, guns blazing. It'll make you look desperate.

- **A typical story pitch includes the when and where (with a twist), the set up, the second-act climax and the resolution.** Don't worry about giving away the ending of your story. If they like it, they'll read it.

- **When attending a film festival don't forget to**: see tons of films, meet craploads of people, ask folks about their projects, and attend as many panels and

Q&A's as you can.

- **Focus on collecting the names of as many producers, agents, and development folks as you can.** If you can't make it to the festival in person, try to catch the archived recording and you can pilfer the contacts that way.

Chapter 6:
"Friending" Your Way to the Top

"A professional writer is an amateur who didn't quit."

-Richard Bach

Maybe I'm a bad person. But I hate Facebook.

I hate how people share what they had for lunch or how "blessed" they are to have found a parking space at the mall.

Or how they think every single thing their dog or child does is unbearably cute – "Pics attached!"- or how I'm the worst person on the face of the Earth if I don't help them win some stupid, mindless game by sending them "crystals" or "credits" or "magic emeralds" or some other bullshit.

That being said...

Social networking is one of the most ninja marketing tools a screenwriter can use.

"I Gave Her My Heart, and She Gave Me a Pen"

Used to be you'd have to spend hours writing, you know, actual letters to every distant cousin and college roommate asking if they knew anybody that worked in the entertainment business.

Today, you can send out a quick status update to your 200 or so "friends" – "Just finished my "Endless Zombie Love" horror spec! Drinks are on me!" - or tweet your100 or so followers your romantic comedy/rock opera is done.

And before you know it, your script is on Wes Craven's desk, all because his daughter plays "Mafia Wars" with your ex-girlfriend's Pilates instructor's life coach.

And though I hate the term "leverage"—(sounds like something you'd hear a CNBC anchor say) — using social networks like Facebook, YouTube and Twitter can save you a crap load of time and get your script through the gatekeepers of Hollywood quicker than a Michael Bay steadicam shot.

But, like voice overs, most writers have no idea how to use them.

"You Realize, Of Course, That We Could Never Be Friends"

There are three social networking tools you should focus on:

- Twitter
- Facebook
- YouTube

I know there's a ton more out there, with quirky names like Zzork and TumblePie and BlooberTron, but they are, mostly, worthless. These three are the big players where most people spend their free time.

Tweet This!

Twitter is the easiest social media tool to master because, with its short 140-character limit, it's little more than a glorified sandwich board.

It can also be a huge waste of time if you're not careful. Here are a couple of things I've learned from my twitter dealings:

Twitter Tip No.1: Follow to Be Followed

I know, it's spammy and unethical, right? To just mass-follow people so they'll follow you back?

Yeah. But it totally works.

If there's a group of people you'd like to target, such as agents or producers or directors, then look at who they follow. Then follow that user's followers.

For instance, if I want to target up-and-coming actors, then I'd follow casting directors.

If I wanted to target new feature directors, I'd

target existing directors like Jon Favreau or Ron Howard, or maybe the twitter handle for a certain high-end digital camera manufacturer.

If I wanted to go after agents, I'd follow @PrinceOfDarkness. (Kidding. Sort of.)

Now this assumes you will tweet out cool stuff, not just spam people. (If you want to do that, this isn't the book for you.)

Don't EVER use automated tools to follow people — ones that do all the following for you overnight. They suck and will get your account banned.

And if somebody follows you, don't un-follow them. (That's just bad mojo.)

Here's a twitter-following formula I use:

- Follow 50 or so people three times a week.

- Wait three days. If they don't follow you back, un-follow them.

- Rinse and repeat.

I find about 30 percent of people you follow will automatically follow you back, so you'll have a thousand followers in no time. Which means a thousand more people that might get your script on a producer's desk.

Twitter Tip No.2: Tweet Funny Stuff, Not Your Own Shit

Don't bug people to read your script or beg them to introduce you to Harvey Weinstein. Send out funny links to stuff about the business. Or cool photos. Or links to weird videos. Anything that gives people a little break from their stressed-out lives.

Some social media gurus advise you to keep the self-promotional stuff down to 25 percent of your overall tweets. I think you should strive for more of an 80/20 mix. (80 percent fun stuff, 20 percent self-promotional.) This means for every five tweets, you're allowed to send out one that's about you.

And when you finally ask for something like, "Anybody know a producer who's looking for a quirky comedy about South Dakota politics?"

They're more likely to not just help...but they could actually be interested in reading your script!

Twitter Tip No.3: Stick to a Schedule

Tweeting once a day is okay, but 2-3 times a day, or more, is ideal. Remember, during the day, people are busy.

So send out funny pictures and short stuff during the day and leave the long videos and blog posts for the evening.

Note: Re-tweeting other people's tweets is probably the best way to get their attention. (We're a vain species. Especially in southern California.)

No.4: Go for the Gold on Sunday Night

Sunday nights, about 5:30 PST, is like prime time Super Bowl viewing for twitter. So make sure you target your quest for help around that time to reach the most people.

Just make sure you do so in a non-threatening, self-deprecating way. Make it fun to help you. (And people usually will.)

Facebook: Where "Friend" Is a Verb

Facebook is the 1000-lb. gorilla of social networks. It's also the one social network people feel most protective about.

Unlike Twitter, Facebook is like a private clubhouse where the kids want to keep anybody out who doesn't belong. So you've gotta tread carefully.

However, for building connections, Facebook can be staggeringly effective. Here are some best practices for screenwriters using Facebook:

Facebook Tip No.1: Go Friend Crazy

Add as many new connections as you possibly can. If you're in a film class, add everybody you can. If you're in a writer's group, add them. If you meet somebody on a laptop at Starbucks working on a script, add them.

Facebook Tip No.2: Use What Ya Got

Scour your existing social network to see if they have connections based in New York, L.A., or London. Chances are, they know "somebody" in the business. One quality referral can be worth more than 25 cold email queries.

Tip No.3: Think About THEM First

Give before you get. As with Twitter, post a lot of cool stuff before you get all clingy and ask for something. Once a day is usually good for Facebook; any more can turn people off.

Facebook Tip No.4: Let Fans Inside

Share your writing process with people. This will make people feel connected to your writing success.

If you've got a question about something your characters might or might not do, ask your Facebook crew. People just love to answer questions on Facebook, so for God sakes let them!

By the time you're ready to circulate your script,

people in your network might just know somebody who can do for you than give you a "like."

Facebook Tip No.5: Power of a Good Question

Ask questions. Don't plead for help. Instead of saying, "I want to sell my script," instead say, "Anybody have any advice on how to get a horror comedy script read?" See how one seems self-serving, and the other seems like a puzzle for the brain to solve?

YouTube, We All Tube

Ah…YouTube. The land of piano-playing cats and bad Justin Bieber covers.

I can't tell you exactly how putting a video on YouTube can transform your career.

But YouTube is the second most popular search engine in the world — not just video site, but search engine. So, if you want eyeballs, and lots, you can find them on YouTube.

And a cool, interesting video can go viral much quicker than anything you could spend years writing. ("South Park" came to the attention of Comedy Central as a viral video passed around by Fox development executives.)

So here are a few YouTube strategies that might pay off:

YouTube Tip No.1: Video Your Pitch

If you've finished your script, and registered it with the WGA, put your pitch on YouTube. (A cool way to do it might be with sock puppets or action figures.) Just don't take yourself too seriously.

YouTube Tip No.2: Webisodes

If you've got film-making skill, why not film shorts each week to show off your writing chops? Not only is it a great way to boost your skills, but it can also be a calling card to getting your script read.

YouTube Tip No.3: Be Funny

Can you do funny movie reviews that people would subscribe to? Can you tell funny stories about your grandma working her DVD player? Can you pull off a satire of popular movies that suck? Try some crazy, off-the-wall strategies. You'd be surprised by what might pay off.

YouTube Tip No. 4: Create Your Own Trailer

Why wait for the studio marketing department to abuse your script? With a decent film-editing software suite, you could throw together a trailer for your script in a couple hours. You could even add in casting ideas and a couple lines from your script.

Just make sure you don't cast Natalie Portman in your project. She's mine, dammit!

Chapter 6 Key Takeaways:

- **Social media isn't just a major time suck.** Twitter, YouTube, and Facebook can be a ninja way to find people to read your script.

- **Tweet out funny, interesting stuff — that doesn't promote and helps other people — 80% of the time.** The rest of the 20% can be tweets asking industry folks to help you.

- **To get tons of Twitter followers, find Twitter accounts you think your IDEAL reader would follow — and then mass follow those followers.** Give 'em three days to follow you back, if not un-follow them.

- **Start your Facebook promotion off by asking your existing social network if they know anybody in L.A., London or New York.** Or any other film industry hub.

- **Share anecdotes of your writing process with your fans**. Keep it positive and upbeat.

- **If you aren't terrified of being on camera, YouTube can be an interesting add to your promotional mix**. You could create a video pitch, put up a trailer of your script, or even do a stand-alone webisode series showcasing your skills.

Chapter 7:
Why Agents and Managers Suck,
Except the Ones That Don't

"The greatest thing in this world is not so much where we are, but in what direction we are moving."

-Oliver Wendell Holmes

Simon was seventeen years old when I met him. He was a resident at a youth detention center in South London when I met him.

And he hadn't said a word in two years.

I was living in London a penniless, desperate American looking for a job. So I took a gig teaching creative writing to "troubled youths full of shite," as my job centre counselor put it.

During the last of our twelve classes, I asked if anybody had any questions. When Simon raised his hand, the class went eerily quiet.

Was he going to thank me for helping him tap into his creative muse?

Did he want to express the pain of growing up in a run-down council flat in Clapham?

Would he talk about the redemptive power of art?

No. Instead, he asked: "Oy, mate! How do I get me an agent?"

That's right. Even miscreant youths who (allegedly) stab their fathers with a kitchen knife over a Chelsea/Arsenal match want to know how to get an agent.

And the number one question I get from screenwriters, without fail, is always: "How do I get an agent?"

The answer: The moment you don't need one.

Agents

Agents make deals. Agents handle bidding wars. Agents negotiate contracts. Agents get you meetings.

They are not for jump-starting your career.

That's because most established agents are trying to get jobs for their existing clients. (You know, the ones who make a living in this business.)

They don't have time, or the motivation, to shepherd and cultivate your talent into a marketable asset. They're too busy getting their own clients to give up on their passion projects and write something marketable.

Most agents don't want to touch you until your material has "talent" attached.

And "talent" means people way more famous than you.

Junior Agents

Now, a lot of screenwriting gurus will tell you to get on the phone and call every agency in town, asking who the junior agents are and who's taking on new clients.

And while I would never dissuade you from trying anything — remember: "Be open to everything..." — I know nobody whose career got started by calling up and asking for representation.

Sure, once you've become a finalist for the Nicholl Fellowship, or you've got a hot commercial director interested in your project, you can get a junior agent at a boutique agency on the phone.

But when you're a nobody, agents don't want to put the time into making you somebody. (They'll let a producer do that.)

So feel free. Knock yourself out. Contact every agent you can. (Just make sure you do all the other stuff in this book too.)

Managers

Managers are like the designated hitter in baseball. Everyone's got an opinion. And everybody thinks the other side is full of crap.

Some screenwriters swear by their managers, claim they never could have reached the success they did without the support of their manager.

Others think they're hucksters, swindling writers out of their hard-earned money.

Here's the scoop: anybody can be a manager.

All you need is a business card. Unlike agents, who need to be licensed by the state. (Head over to http://scriptbully.com/wga for a list of agents from the Writer's Guild of America (WGA).)

That doesn't mean there aren't some great writer managers out there. But I find managers beneficial when taking your career to the next level -- shifting from feature to TV, moving from rom-com to action, going from writer to writer/producer.

Not when you're trying to find any level at all. But please, get out there and show me wrong.

I dare ya.

A Final Note on Representation

As much as I bash agents and managers, and there's quite a bit to bash, they are a crucial part of your submission strategy.

Because to reach the talent (actors, directors) you need to talk to their "people." And their "people" are managers and agents.

Just don't expect them to become "your" people. At least not until you sell that action spec about giant squids attacking Denver for mid-six figures.

Chapter 7 Key Takeaways:

- **Every writer thinks they need an agent or manager to represent them to get their career started.** When really they NEED the agent or manager of a director or actor.

- **Managers can be a boost to your screenwriting career, but be careful...anybody can be an agent.** Managers are often best added to your team once your career gets up and running.

Chapter 8:
Schmoozing the Gatekeepers

"Always do what you are afraid to do."

-Ralph Waldo Emerson

At this point you should have hundreds of RELEVANT industry contacts you can reach out to.

Again, I said "relevant."

If you're writing a comedy spec, a producer who specializes in horror should not be at the top of your list.

If you're shopping a family-friendly feature, a production company that does nothing but soft-core adult fare like "Really Magic Mike" or "Seduction Island" probably isn't your best bet.

But if you've followed the steps outlined in this

book, you should have contact info for at least 100-150 people stuffed into your spreadsheet. (If not, go back and do more digging until you come up with at least that many.)

Then it's time to begin your blitz.

"You've Got Mail"

So you've got list of whom to contact. But what does "contact" mean?

I won't belabor the point — too late? — but you need to focus your time and energy on email queries. Query letters are not the way things are done. (Anymore.)

And what should be in your email query?

The template is simple. And short. Here's an example using "Bridesmaids":

Subject Line:

"Available Thriller" or *"Available Comedy"* or

"Available Horror" or if you're contacting a talent's manager or agent: "Re: Christopher Nolan"

Email Body:

I have an available script.

"The Hangover" meets "Bride Wars," set in the dangerous, backstabbing world of bridesmaid dresses and catered rehearsal dinners.

Would you like to see it?

Michael Rogan
(310-225-xxxx)

That's it. You are not pitching. You are not detailing your story beats or sending a treatment.

Or describing that heartwarming scene in the second act when little Timmy learns to walk again after a devastating Go-gurt accident.

You're fishing for a bite, not a three-course meal. Either they're looking or they aren't.

No point in going on and on about your story if they don't have the remotest interest in your project.

And by doing it this way, you'll set yourself apart by:

- Showing you know how this industry works by helping "frame" your story by comparing it to previous projects.

- Demonstrating you understand how busy they are by getting to the frickin' point.

- Giving them a chance to "see" where your script fits into their plans.

And if they can "see" how your material aligns with their needs they are much likely to look.

"My Baby, She Wrote Me a Letter"

So you've got your spreadsheet full of emails. It's now time to hit SEND!

Please, whatever you do. Send them individually.

Not only do you risk being labeled a spammer by your ISP if you send them en masse, but you're more likely to make a catastrophic email mistake if you send out 250 emails at a time.

Just send out 15-20 emails every couple of hours. You'll be through that list in no time.

Then what? One of four things:

- They reply, saying if you email them again they'll file a restraining order.

- They reply, saying "not interested."

- They don't respond.

- They send you a release so you can send the script in.

If it's the first response, take them off your list.

(No reason to piss anybody off in this town.)

And the last one is easy: SEND THE FRICKIN' SCRIPT.

But the middle two are more delicate. What do you do if they reject your project, but don't reject you outright?

Keep them on file for a future project. (But don't bug them with this script. They don't want it.)

And what do you do if you get no response?

Well, we then enter the phone call phase of our tactical operation.

"I'm Your Number One Fan"

If I don't hear from somebody I've emailed, I usually give them about two weeks. After that, I'll follow up with a phone call.

Let's talk about phone calls for a minute. Every writer hates them. I know that. Christ, I hate cold calling as much as the next person.

But sometimes we've got to do what we hate. (Like paying taxes, or taking our niece to a "Twilight" movie.)

The key thing with phone calls is to:

- Relax
- Be cool
- Pretend like the person we're calling is expecting our call

It's hard to muster up confidence to call a total stranger. So, if that's difficult for you, just remember how awesome your script is. Focus on that and keep your own weird neuroses out of it.

Anatomy of a Perfect Phone Call

The purpose of a phone call is not to simply be patched through to a decision-maker. (Though that's a nice side benefit.)

The real purpose is to be perceived as a person, not just a nuisance to be dealt with.

And you do that by being approachable, calm and funny (if you can).

So here's my little formula for calling and getting through the gatekeepers. It breaks down something like this:

- The hello

- The reason you're calling

- The real reason you're calling

- The funny grovel

- The end around

Here's a sample script of how it might go down:

Receptionist: Thanks for calling the Abrams Agency. This is Jennifer. How may I direct your call?

Me: Hi, Jennifer. Can I speak to Jim Abrams, please? He should be expecting my call. My name is Michael Rogan and I'm a screenwriter. *(The Hello)*

Receptionist: Mr. Rogan, can I ask what this is regarding?

Me: I have a writing project I wanted to discuss with Jim. *(The reason I'm calling)*

Receptionist: Mr. Abrams doesn't discuss projects over the phone.

Me: Oh, I totally understand. It's just that I think this project would be absolutely perfect for his client, Scarlett Johansson. *(The "real" reason I'm calling: I've done my homework. I know what he wants. I know who his clients are.)*

Receptionist: I'm sorry, I don't think that will be possible.

Me: I get it. And usually I wouldn't even call. But it would take just one minute of his time and I'm like 97 percent sure he'd love it. I'd even maybe go as high as 98 percent. *(Funny grovel)*

Receptionist: Sorry, Mr. Rogan, that won't be

possible.

Me: Jennifer, I know you've got a job to do. And you're doing it great. Is there anybody else there at the agency that could spare a minute and might be interested in hearing about this project? I'd really appreciate any help you could give. *(The end around)*

Receptionist: Well...I'm not supposed to....Hold on, let me check.

Me: Thank you, Jennifer. Will you marry me?

Note: You don't have to do the engagement part. (Unless you want to.)

Here are a few takeaways regarding the phone script:

I don't mention the email query. Why would I mention the fact I've already been dissed? The gatekeeper need not know "why" he's expecting my call. Just that he is.

I refer to it as a "project," not a "script." This makes it sound less desperate, and more like something her boss would want to hear about.

I constantly show her I hear what she's saying, a huge key to effective communication. But then, I gently keep requesting to be patched through again and again. (In a really polite way.)

I try to make him/her laugh. This can often be the factor that sways receptionists and secretaries to patch you through.

I'm genuinely nice to them. This IS the most important factor to getting put through.

I don't pitch them my story idea like some meth addict. Don't do this. It's not the way things are done.

I give her many opportunities to say yes, without appearing a complete loon.

I give her the chance to "help" at the end. This makes her slightly invested. (And hopefully willing to help.)

"Red Five, Standing By"

And what do you do if you actually do get patched through to somebody? Deliver your super-short pitch as we went over in Chapter 4.

Here's my formula for finally talking to a decision-maker on the phone:

- The thank you

- The reason you're calling

- The elevator pitch

- The request

Sounds something like this:

"Hi there,

Thanks for taking my call. (The thank you)

I've written a screenplay I think might be perfect for you and/or your client. (The reason you're calling)

It's about an Irish Catholic priest in suburban Boston

*who takes on a ruthless Boston crime lord. His estranged
father. (The pitch)*

Would you like me to send you a copy?" (The request)

Don't linger, don't break out all your beats. They
will let you know if they're interested.

And really punch the "irony" aspect of your
script. (It's what makes your story memorable.)

Chapter 8 Key Takeaways:

- **Forget query letters.** It's all about email now.

- **Keep your subject line simple and short.** Example: "Available Horror Comedy Script" or "Re: Megan Fox Horror Project."

- **Don't pitch your entire story in your email.** Just give 'em a taste of the genre, similar movies and maybe a note about what makes your story unique.

- **Be sure to send out email queries one at a time.** You are not selling insurance…you're selling art, dammit!

- **If they don't get back to or say "not interested" then it's time to jump on the phone.** Scary, but effective.

- **Be nice and self-deprecating to administrative staff when calling**. Tell them the industry bigwig is expecting your call and you're hoping to speak to them about a "project." (Never call it a script.)

- **You won't get through to everybody, but when you do give them your short elevator pitch**. Rehearse this a ton so it comes off as confident and relaxed.

Chapter 9:
Submissions, Submissions, Submissions

"The toughest part of getting to the top of the ladder is getting through the crowd at the bottom."

-Anonymous

So you've gotten somebody to bite on your script? Fantastic!

Now the key is not to royally screw it up by looking like some stalker.

Here is what you need to know:

Submission Tip No.1: Send it...Now!

You'd be shocked to learn how many people wait a day or two to send their script. (Maybe they don't want to seem desperate. Who the hell knows?)

Don't wait. Do it now. Waiting a day or two, they might forget you exist.

Submission Tip No.2: Put "As Requested By…" in Email Subject Line

You'll be emailing the script and scanning the release, so be sure to have something in there that says this item was actually requested and is not some random cold submission.

Submission Tip No. 3: Sign The Release

You have no idea how many crazy people out there sue development folks. And I know you're absolutely convinced film-biz types are primed to take your premise about a killer penguin ninja squad and turn them into a trilogy of bestselling movies and theme parks.

But it's way cheaper for them to buy your script outright. (Besides your idea probably isn't that great. So, don't worry.)

Submission Tip No.4: Keep It Simple

No decorations. No frilly script covers. No pictures. No graphs, no charts. No nothing, except for a title page and the script.

Submission Tip No.5: Tell 'Em Who You Are

Write a brief message in the body of your reply email reminding them of your phone conversation.

"Hey, Jim. Thanks for speaking to me on the phone. Here's the script you requested. Look forward to hearing from you."

Keep it short, but again make it clear to the person processing the email this is a requested property.

Submission Tip No.6: Give Up Your Digits

Put your contact info on the title page. Don't assume your script and your short note will be married together.

If things go well, your script will be copied for tons of people to look at. This is a good thing. Make sure they know how to find you.

Submission Tip No.7: Don't Cheat

Don't make your 135-page western look like it's 102 pages by adjusting the margins, or reducing the size of the font. Industry people know all the tricks. (Because they've pulled off most of them at some point.) If your script is too long, cut it.

Chapter 9 Key Takeaways:

- **If your industry contact wants to read your script, SEND your script!** Don't wait. Do it now.

- **Put "As Requested By" on the envelope or subject of the email when sending back the script.** Otherwise it'll get lost in the slush pile.

- **Sign the release.** Don't worry about somebody stealing your idea. It's easier to BUY your script, than plagiarize it.

- **Don't add stupid decorations or frilly crap along with your script.** Keep it simple and professional.

Chapter 10:
The Strange and Mysterious World of Meetings

"Make us laugh or cry, and we'll get you a deal. Make us do both and we'll get you an auction."

-Andrea Brown

After somebody reads your script, you'll get one of three responses (assuming you get a response):

- They will reject you.

- They will buy your script on the spot.

- They will ask to meet with you.

If they want to buy your script, get an entertainment lawyer. Not your Uncle Stanley who does most of his business in traffic court.

And stop reading this book. You're officially over the gates. (This Jedi master has nothing left to teach you.)

But if they want to meet with you, this is also good. It means they're not quite ready to marry you without going on a date first.

"First You Want to Kill Me, Now You Want to Kiss Me"

The only thing I know writers hate more than making phone calls is taking meetings.

I have no idea why. They're fun when you think about it.

Somebody in the film business asks you to come in and talk about...you! (What could be better than that?)

Here's the cool thing, if they want you to "come to town" in L.A., NY or London, you can contact every other producer, manager and agent on your list by saying:

"Hi Sam,

I'm gonna be in town April 23rd- April 25th taking a few meetings regarding my script "NAVY Seal Ninja Squad 5."

I'll be at ICM a good part of Tuesday, but I'm free Wednesday or Thursday if you have an opening in your schedule."

What rep or producer wouldn't respond to that? ("He's meeting at ICM. Crap! Get him on the phone!")

Sneaky tactic: But what if you didn't have a meeting yet? Notice I didn't say I'm meeting with somebody at ICM. I just said I'll "be at ICM" (They have a great picnic area.)

It's dodgy, but a tactic that may be worth trying. If they ask WHO you're meeting with, for a name, just say it's with 2-3 agents in the motion picture lit department.

"The Bottom is Loaded With Nice People"

Every meeting is different. Sometimes you'll be asked to come in to talk about your spec.

Other times they like your spec, but they want you to come in and pitch other ideas. (If so, be prepared with at least five killer ideas.)

Sometimes they may want you to rewrite another writer's work.

And other times, it'll just be a "get to know you" meeting, where they're interested in representing you or working with you, but want to make sure you're not a psychopath.

Here are a few tips to keep in mind before you head out on your first meeting:

Meeting Tip No.1: Be on Time

Or better yet, be a half-hour early. Driving five miles in L.A., NY or London can take thirty minutes. Prepare accordingly.

Meeting Tip No.2: Dress Like You Give a Shit

Don't wear hats or jeans with holes in them. Dress nice, but not like it's high school graduation. Casual, but cool.

Meeting Tip No.3: Get Personal

Scan the office for small-talk topics. Are they a Clippers fan or a Lakers fan? Are there framed albums of Aerosmith in the office? Do they have a somewhat inappropriate devotion to scrapbooking?

Find something you can riff on and start there. Build rapport.

Meeting Tip No.4: Don't START With Your Story

Start with your connection to the material. Don't dive into your pitch.

Go with: "I was at the DMV one day and I thought, "What if we had no cars and had to go back to riding horses? And so I came up with 'Horsing Around'..." This is a great way to move onto the pitch and give the folks insight on whether they want to work with you.

Meeting Tip No.5: Make sure YOU end the meeting.

Don't wait for the hook to pull you off stage. Say you've got another meeting across town. Whatever. Don't linger. They probably need to talk shit about you behind your back before they give you an answer.

Meeting Tip No.6: Know What You Like

Before you dig into the heart of your meeting, there'll be an icebreaker portion of the meeting. You'll be asked questions like "what are your favorite movies" or "what did you think of the (latest film in your genre)." It would be extra helpful if you had an opinion, or had seen a movie in the last, say, two years.

Meeting Tip No.7: Know What You're Working On

If they ask you what you're working on, don't say: "Nothing. I'm currently living in my mother's basement and building up my collection of vintage action figures." Tell them what's on your plate. Even if it's just research for your next project.

Meeting Tip No.8: Know the Etiquette

If you're asked if you'd like water, or if you'd like your parking validated, say yes. It's okay to be a human, with human concerns like hydration and parking. But don't ask for a Limited Edition Dasani collected from rainwater at the base of a Himalayan mountain. You want to seem casual, not neurotic.

Chapter 10 Key Takeaways:

- **If film-industry folks want you to come into town for a meeting, be sure to schedule a few more to make the most of your time.** Leverage your existing meeting to get more bang for your meeting buck.

- **Prepare for your meetings.** Both in dress and material.

- **Research who the meeting will be with and come up with icebreakers to begin the meeting.** Don't just jump into rambling about your story idea.

- **After small talk, phase into WHY you're connected to the material.** This will get them emotionally involved first.

- **Be honest, but not too honest.** Don't

bash other filmmakers unless it's Michael Bay.

- **Tell 'em what else you're working on**. Try to come up with 2-3 other story ideas before heading into the meeting.

- **Try to end the meeting before they do**. Be polite, but don't linger like you have no other place to be.

- **Have fun**. Relax. And kick some serious ass.

Epilogue: "The Beginning of a Beautiful Friendship"

I'm not going to pretend I'm an agent. (I have a moral compass.)

But when somebody wants to work with you to either:

- Option your script (Where they pay you money to go shop your material)

- Buy your script

- Hire you off of a pitch

- Hire you to do a rewrite

- Hire you to do ANYTHING

Then it's time to call in the big guns. And that's when you can, suddenly, get every agency in town on the phone.

Forget emails, just call up.

Me: *"Hi, my name is Michael Rogan and I'm a screenwriter with a pending deal with a production company. I wonder if there are any agents taking on new clients who I could talk to."*

Receptionist: *"Sure. Uh...yes. Right away sir!"*

At this point, you're in the driver's seat. You do the interviewing.

You listen to THEIR pitch and choose who you feel most comfortable with. Don't worry, you'll probably end up firing your first agent anyway.

"We All Prisoners, Chickee-Baby"

But once you do make that sale, or get that job, it's time to celebrate.

And thank all the friends and family who supported you and helped you along the way. (Maybe even thank those who didn't support you. Revenge is fun.)

Enjoy this moment. Really. Throw a HUGE party and savor this moment.

Because you haven't so much crossed a finish line, as you've started a new race.

This triathlon requires two careers: kick-ass writing and kick-ass marketing.

Your agents and managers will help open doors, but you've gotta deliver once you walk through the door.

You've got to keep writing specs even when you're not paid for it. You've got to keep up on who got fired from which studio and which star just out of rehab needs your zombie romantic comedy spec.

You've got to continue to use the techniques in this book - going to festivals, using Twitter and Facebook, calling up producers, seeing lots of movies - more than ever.

Because everybody roots for the underdog. But once you're in the castle, once you've penetrated the impenetrable walls of the film business, you're just another writer other writers hate.

"Please, Sir. I Want Some More"

I remember optioning my first script for five thousand dollars. (A romantic comedy that wasn't funny or romantic.)

And I thought my life had changed.

For three months, I hung out in my apartment in Carlsbad, California feeling like the most talented being on the face of the earth.

I would scoff at movies I felt were below my esteemed skill. I told women in seedy bars that I was on the verge of greatness, so they should get my phone number NOW before I became monumentally famous.

I waited for limos full of agents and producers to magically come to my door and whisk me away to a magical land of six-figure development deals and studio-lot offices and champagne-fueled weekends in

Palm Springs with leggy supermodels.

What I didn't do was work my ass off.

I'm not big on regret; I feel it's as unproductive as a Michael Bay sequel.

But if I could talk to that young guy, I'd say shut the F@## up. And get back to work.

If I had, I might be writing to you today from my Hollywood Hills mansion where Snoop Dogg is my neighbor. (Or I'd be working the night shift at a 7-11 in Palmdale. Who knows?)

So, if you make a sale. Please. Send me a note at michael@scriptbully.com. I'll frame it and put it on the wall.

I'll raise a glass of champagne for you. And then I'll tell you, as nicely as I can, get the f#$#$ back to work.

Good luck with your writing. And if you've enjoyed this book, drop me a line at Michael@scriptbully.com.

Appendix: Or All Those Resources We Mentioned

Chapter One:

- IMDb Pro – ScriptBully.com/imdbpro
  ScriptBully.com/moonstruck
- Google Voice- Google.com/Voice
- "Raising Arizona" –
  ScriptBully.com/Arizona

Chapter Two:

- ScriptReader Services – email me at
  michael@scriptbully.com with
  SCRIPTREADER in subject line

Chapter Five:

- Austin Film Festival/Screenwriting
  Conference (Austin, TX) -
  http://www.austinfilmfestival.com/

- Nashville Screenwriting Conference
  (Nashville, TN) -
  http://www.nashscreen.com/

- Toronto Screenwriting Conference (Toronto, ON) - http://www.torontoscreenwritingconference.com/

- Stonybrook Summer Conference (Stony Brook, NY) - http://www.stonybrook.edu/sb/mfa/summer/screenwriting/

- Sundance Film Festival - http://www.sundance.org/festival/

- Telluride Film Festival - http://telluridefilmfestival.org/

- South by Southwest http://sxsw.com/

- Slamdance Film Festival http://www.slamdance.com/

- Austin Film Festival http://www.austinfilmfestival.com/

- Tribeca Film Festival http://www.tribecafilm.com/festival/

Don't Forget:
A Special FREE Gift for You!

If you'd like FREE instant access to my seminar "7 Secrets to a Kick-Ass and Marketable Screenplay" then head over to **ScriptBully.com/Free**. (What else you gonna do? Watch another "Twilight" movie?!)

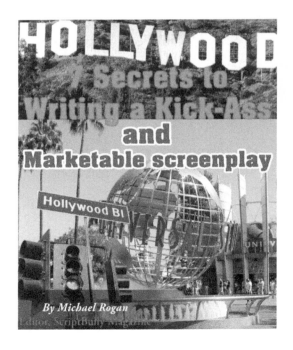

Made in the USA
Coppell, TX
25 October 2023

23384200R00080